Smile, or Else

Smile or else

Winner of the 2021 Press 53 Award for Poetry

Chanel Brenner

Press 53
———◆———
Winston-Salem

Press 53, LLC
PO Box 30314
Winston-Salem, NC 27130

First Edition

A Tom Lombardo Poetry Selection

Cover image, "Smoking Candle," Copyright © 2020
by Bernd Schmidt
Liscensed through iStock

Cover design by Claire V. Foxx and Kevin Morgan Watson

.

Library of Congress Control Number
2021932317

Printed on acid-free paper
ISBN 978-1-950413-34-8

Grateful acknowledgment is made to the editors of the following publications in which these poems, or previous versions, first appeared:

All We Can Hold: poems of motherhood: "Sun"
Barren Magazine: "At the Hair Salon"
Barrow Street: "Sleepover"
Carnival Magazine: "Desmond's Eyes"
Chiron Review: "On the Anniversary of Your Son's Death"
Cider Press Review: "When My Yoga Teacher Tells Me I'm Vata Deranged" & "Clear-Cut"
Crosswinds Poetry Journal: "Desmond's Older Brother Is"
Deep Water Literary Journal: "Back at the El Encanto"
Door Is a Jar Magazine: "The Tug of War"
Duende: "God's Hand," "Raising Grief," and "When Desmond Asks, Am I Born to Play Football?"
Enizagam: "When They Call to Tell You Your Son Is Dying"
Glass: A Journal of Poetry: "The Morning Before the Pregnancy Test"
Great Weather for Media: "Chopsticks"
Literary Mama: "Mother Trucker"
Mothers Always Write: "I Want to Be Kind to My Seven-Year-Old Son"
Muzzle Magazine: "After" and "While Cleaning the Play Room"
New Ohio Review: "El Día de los Muertos"
Pittsburgh Poetry Review: "At a Restaurant the Night My Son Died"
Rattle: "To the Frustrated Mother at Starbucks with Her Three-Year-Old Son"
Salamander Magazine: "What I'm Holding in the Black and White Photo of Me and My First-Born Son"
Slippery Elm: "A Hail Mary," "Night Bleed," and "What I Miss"
Smartish Pace: "Reflection"
Spoon River Poetry Review: "We Never Heal, Just Remember Less"
Switchback Journal: "Facebook Post: Mother Son Hike at Solstice Canyon," "Thinnest Day of the Year," and "Welcome to Dead Child World"
The Midnight Oil: "Hard-Boiled Eggs"
West Trade Review: "What We Choose to Believe"
West Trestle Review: "Something Has Lifted"

Contents

I.

At a Restaurant the Night My Son Died   3
El Día de los Muertos   4
Welcome to Dead Child World   5
What I Miss   6
Hard-Boiled Eggs   7
Speaking of Teeth   9
A Hail Mary   11
After   12
Something Has Lifted   13
Sun   15
Chopsticks   16
On the Anniversary of Your Son's Death   18
Desmond's Eyes   19

II.

Back at the *El Encanto*   23
The Morning Before the Pregnancy Test   24
Turning Seven   25
When They Call to Tell You Your Son Is Dying   26
The Tug of War   27
Desmond's Permanent Tooth   29
At Sequin Boutique   31
Facebook Post: Mother Son Hike at Solstice Canyon
    183 Likes   32
We Never Heal, Just Remember Less   33
Ode to the Crossing Guard at 25th & Pearl   34
Night Bleed   35
What I'm Holding in the Black and White Photo of Me
    and My First-Born Son   37
Sleepover   38
What We Choose to Believe   40
Mustela Baby Wipes   42
I Want to Be Kind to My Seven-Year-Old Son   43

III.

At the Hair Salon Today 47
Desmond's Older Brother Is 48
While Cleaning the Playroom 49
When Desmond Asks, *Am I Born to Play Football?* 50
Proxy 51
Thinnest Day of the Year 52
Raising Grief 53
Mother Trucker 54
Reflection 56
God's Hand 57
Clear-Cut 58
A Different Clock 59
To the Frustrated Mother in Starbucks with Her
   Three-Year-Old Son 61
When My Yoga Teacher Tells Me I'm Vata Deranged 63

Acknowlegments 65

Author Biography 67

I.

At a Restaurant the Night My Son Died

I sat across from Riley,
shooting his portrait with my phone.

His charcoal sweatshirt faded
into the dark booth.

He played tic-tac-toe
in the dim light.

I should have known
something was wrong,

when he scribbled his *X's* and *O's*
like a toddler—

should have known
his brain's weak vessels . . .

his arteriovenous
malformations . . .

were bleeding again.
Should have put down the phone

and looked him in the eye.
Should have noticed

his half-eaten ice cream
melting in the bowl.

El Día de los Muertos

was Riley's favorite holiday.

He loved smelling the sugar skulls,

didn't mind that he couldn't eat them.

My husband asks, *Who wants a dead kid's bike?*

then places Riley's in the alley for someone to take.

Some believe the dead are insulted by sorrow.

My husband rummages through boxes in our garage

like we are having a fire sale.

He finds my dead father's rare coins in a sock,

a card from my dead grandmother.

In Riley's closet, I absorb the silent, airless church of his clothes,

and realize sugar skulls have space on the forehead for a name.

My husband runs outside to retrieve Riley's bike.

Welcome to Dead Child World

Please try to make yourself comfortable even though you are outside your body. Don't worry, this is as normal as a cocoon. Part of you crossed over with your child, and what remains is a shell. Refrain from catching your fleeting reflection in mirrors or windows. A new you will emerge, but not today. The woman will knock on your door with ashes in a plastic box, tucked inside a baby blue gift bag. It will remind you of a shower gift. If your dead child had a brother or sister younger than three, tell them repeatedly, *No he's not in the hospital. No, he's not coming home. No, he's not going to be born again.* Firmly, in the same tone every time, without tears. If you chose to donate your child's organs, remember that his heart, liver, and kidneys will eventually die. The label, *Parent of a Dead Child*, is necessary. Wear it conspicuously, so other parents will know to avoid your contagion.

What I Miss

A chrysalis hangs in the vines,
then a butterfly.
Somehow I miss them both.

I don't see
the wisteria blooming
outside my bedroom window,
because I don't open the shade.

I see the Mylar balloon
my husband bought
for my birthday,
an oversized cake with arms, legs,
and a lemon-slice smile.

That was the summer
I stood in our yard
watering the dead grass,
humming birds buzzing
through the spray.
I watched the smiling balloon
drift out our open back door,
and vanish in the stratus.

Hard-Boiled Eggs

Riley is dead,
and now, I make eggs
for his brother, Desmond,
like I used to do
for him.

As I boil the water,
I remember how Riley loved
to shift them,
in the glass bowl
while they cooled,
watching light
flicker the water,

as if he beheld a world,
unknown to me.

Riley gliding
like the eggs,
through silken water,
back into
the embryo's shell—
the membrane so sheer,
a ray of light
must have beckoned him.

Sometimes, I imagine
him on the other side
of that veiled split,
or in another kitchen,
staring at eggs
knowing
he's unable to grasp.

I drop the hardboiled eggs
in a bowl of cold water,
submerge my hand,
and sway the ovals
with my fingers.

Their shells clink.
Desmond says,
Church bells.

Speaking of Teeth

Mommy, can I push Desmond
in the stroller?

How his pace quickened
as he thrust the stroller
toward the street,

Yes, Riley, but don't run—

I remember the time he fell
on his two front teeth.

When he started to run,
I yelled, *STOP!*
He did, just before letting go.
The stroller sailed off the steep curb
into the street, and flipped—
Desmond's face crashed
and slid on the asphalt,
his front teeth piercing
his lower lip.

I don't know which was worse—
the blood running
from Desmond's two front teeth,
or the look on Riley's face.

Mommy, I didn't mean. . .
But you did it! I yelled.

Four years later, I watch
a little boy push a stroller
past our house,
as his mother walks beside him.

Desmond's teeth have healed.
Riley is dead.
I still hear his words,

Mommy, I didn't mean to let go.

A Hail Mary

I meet with my grief group friend,
who recently lost
a six-week-old boy.
She chugs hard cider—
Everything just sucks.
I nod, no eloquence needed,
amongst empty baskets of chili fries,
and two dead sons
between us.

After lunch, we spill
onto the crowded boardwalk,
with our two living children.
My six-year-old Desmond tries to teach
her three-year-old daughter
how to throw a football.

When passersby smile,
How sweet! they see us
as two moms enjoying a Sunday
with their children,
vibrant, whole—

unlike the doorman missing
a leg, at Big Dean's Sports Bar,
confiding, *I used to be
an athlete,* as he throws
my son a Hail Mary.

All I can see is
his empty jean leg,
dangling
after its soul is gone.

After

Dust motes linger
in a splinter of sun.

An empty brown mug
awaits Riley's return.

The Black-eyed Gerber daisies
slump in milky water.

A wisp of streamer from his sixth birthday
clings to a still fan blade.

One day, it too, will fall,
twisting like an oak's last leaf.

A white moon appears
out the window,

like an infant's fingernail,
cradled in the womb of the sky.

Something Has Lifted

My husband sprints as if
he could outrun his grief—

through the kitchen,
checking his oversized iPhone,

grabbing his keys,
and most days, his wedding ring,

asking, *Did I kiss you yet?*
before shutting the door.

I miss the smell of French Roast
brewing in our house by the beach,

before we got married
and stopped drinking coffee—

our palm tree swaying in wind,
slowly as our days: toasting bagels,

browsing nurseries, planting
flowers in our rented garden,

having sex, napping—
then pressing *repeat*.

Last night, I watched him play
Transformers with Desmond,

for the first time the way
he used to play with Riley,

ending with a dinosaur
on the floor, legs

surrendered to air.
Today, my husband leans easily

against the kitchen counter,
smiling like he used to,

in our bagel days.
Desmond enters, mirroring

his father's smile, their faces
like two halves

of the same broken geode,
as they clean the toys off the floor.

Sun

The memory of my dead son burns,
like sun breaking

through fog
over Half Moon Bay—

my dead son waiting
behind its gray veil,

playing with my ghost.
He responds,

when my living son laughs,
tickled by my apparition—

my mothering split in two worlds.
When my living son laughs,

my dead son's laugh penetrates like sunlight—
my ghost's memory burning through.

Chopsticks

As a gardener
        trims the lawn
                with a weed cutter,

the smell of grass knifes
        through the narrow opening
                between door and frame.

I live in the future
        of a poem
                I once wrote,

for the eighth anniversary
        of my son Riley's
                death.

I sit, gripping each letter
        of his name
                with chopsticks,

chewing and swallowing,
        savoring each
                severed flavor.

The poem is a kana
        on the wall, a man
                vanishes into stone steps

people keep tripping over
        a broken wine glass,
                someone yelling, *fire*!

I wrap myself
    in Riley's favorite blanket,
        eating rice with a fork.

My toddler, Desmond, sits across from me,
    eating bites of chicken
        with chopsticks.

In the silence
    the smell of grass
        turns to smoke.

On the Anniversary of Your Son's Death

Plan a trip to Hawaii.
Buy non-refundable tickets.
Toss whatever into your suitcase.

Walk past the photo of him
in your arms, and the wooden sail boat
he sanded smooth in kindergarten.

Before you board the plane, drink a margarita.
Order the cheap red wine split in-flight.
Eat the bag of chocolate chip cookies.

Savor the hour-gate-waiting delay at Kahului.
Sway with the palms your window frames.
Ignore the feeling you've forgotten something.

When the woman next to you
answers an urgent call with, *No!*
I just saw him this morning . . . he was fine,

listen to her sob.
Don't avert your eyes when she looks at you.
Breathe the frozen air like an alpine climber.

Desmond's Eyes

I am a boat,
sailing endlessly
in their pacific
blue oceans.

I slip them on
like perfectly fitting gloves,
casting shadow puppets
on the walls.

I dance with them
to the Red Hot Chili Peppers,
preening in the mirror,
like I did at fifteen.

I bounce on their
two trampolines till
I'm breathless and dizzy.

I fall into their featherbeds,
sink into
the imprint of myself,
and never wake
from these dreams.

I pocket them
like two moonstones clinking.

II.

Back at the *El Encanto*

The hotel has aged backwards,
cracks filled in, chipped paint
smoothed, sagging walls lifted.

I almost remember
the younger us, bouncing
like a diamond's
iridescent reflected light,

running through rain,
our tongues sweet
with champagne—

out of focus snapshots
with too much light
or not enough.

At dinner, I see that couple
on a love seat
sharing crème brûlée,
spooning, without looking.

Look at us now,
our image diminished
like a reflection
in a rearview mirror.

The only difference between
then and now is time

and our son's death,
a semi-truck
we didn't see coming
to broadside us.

The Morning Before the Pregnancy Test

Now when I think of veins,
I see death returning.
I try to imagine my belly swelling,
my veins safe in compression hosiery,
but I can't suture what has opened.

My eyelid swells from a spider bite,
till I look like a monster. Other mothers' kids
panic; baby spiders crawl in my veins.
Fear of another bite turns me
wide-eyed and spindly.
I hope to escape my body.

The window cracks open,
the seed in my belly swells,
and I shop once more at Babies R Us—
but I see death monsters everywhere—
and cannot end the panic.

I am a monster. A stone mommy monster,
and only a stone baby monster would want
stone blood in its veins. What if I miscarry
from panic? What if I birth death again?

The defect in my son's brain didn't look
like a monster worthy of such panic.

It looked like a veined apple leaf,
a blueprint for life.

Turning Seven

My birthday is tomorrow!
Desmond says, his face white
with the thick sunscreen
that doesn't give him a rash.

As I slather his beanpole arms,
he asks if we can talk about his party,
to make time go faster, but I want
to slow it—his rosy flesh revealed,
as I rub lotion further into his shoulders.

Only one more day till I'm seven—I try
to keep him still, to hold his slippery wrist—

I've never had a seven-year-old before,
I blurt without thinking.

You're right, he agrees,
looking beyond me, gone

to that faraway place
where he thinks about his brother,
who died at the age of six.

When They Call to Tell You Your Son Is Dying

Go to your vanity
and greet your ghost.

Smooth foundation
onto your ashen face.

Dot concealer on dark
under-eye circles.

You must dust your face
with rice powder,

mark your cheekbones
with *bloodroot.*

Gloss your lashes with mascara,
separate them with a brush.

Paint your lips
with *Afghan red.*

Draw fierce blue lines
around your eyes.

If anyone asks
why you're doing this,

say it's the last time
you will look this alive.

The Tug of War

Having dinner with another couple
who also lost a child,

I watch their two-year-old
bounce on her mother's lap,

tug her mother's face and hair,
while she looks at the menu.

The child is the same age Desmond was
the night Riley died.

The same age as Desmond
when he asked,

If you had another baby,
would it be Riley?

When the mother says
she'll stick with water,

I ask if she's pregnant.
She nods her head,

but no smile tugs her lips.
I've been crying, she says.

I know I should be happy,
and I am, but I'm scared too.

Eleven years ago, when we learned
I was pregnant with Riley,

we bought a crib the same day.
If I became pregnant now,

I don't know what I'd do—
hope pulling one way, grief the other—

joy a rope in my hands,
raw and burning.

Desmond's Permanent Tooth

I chipped my tooth!

Desmond yells from the back seat—

and springs from the car

like a Jack-in-the-box,

before I turn the engine off.

He paces our sidewalk,

hand-over-mouth, body hunched,

You're going to kill me, he worries,

It's my permanent one—

now I panic.

I broke it on my canteen.

I reach for his face,

but he runs to the bathroom,

I want to look in the mirror first.

I catch a glimpse—

a triangular chunk missing,

like a broken seashell.

Fuck! he cries,

as I promise the dentist

will be able to fix it.

Without his glasses, he looks

like his brother,

dead six years, his photo

resting on the stone mantel,

beside a depleted candle.

It's only a tooth, I say.

He nods, bare eyes hopeful,

though we both know it isn't true.

At Sequin Boutique

I wonder, when the owner says,
We're closing at the end of the month,
Do we ever stop feeling hollowed by loss?

I still grieve the lipstick I used in my twenties.
When Lancome discontinued *Matte Claret,*
I stopped at every store for the coveted tubes,
digging my fingernail into the last one,
until it was just an empty hole.

Riley and I loved to shop here, before he died,
and I hear him comment as I sift through shirts,
ogling the rainbow colors and favored sheens.

I stop, distracted by the window's reflection—
a blue shawl draping a manikin's shoulders
more like a rescue blanket, than fashion.
I hear my younger self ask,
echoing from the bottom of a well—
if Riley likes the blouse I'm holding.

He chants, *Mom, get this one,*
this one, this one, as he rubs
the past against his face,
shining in the window like ash.

Facebook Post: Mother Son Hike at Solstice Canyon
183 Likes

Look at our wide smiles, muscular legs, blond hair blowing in wind,

not my clenched jaw, tight neck muscles.

See grassy hills, yellow wildflowers, shades of blue,

not me dragging him away from the Xbox.

Admire the ocean merging with sky,

not the fight in the car,

the sun-kissed earth,

not his complaints of being cold when he wouldn't wear a jacket,

our faces, radiant with dew,

not his car sickness.

See the trail's summit—

not my fear of him falling off the cliff.

Like our heads tilted toward each other,

not someone shouting, "Smile, or else!"

We Never Heal, Just Remember Less

Stretching my legs
after a walk down our old street,

my dead son's face came to me,
the scar below

his left eyebrow, the window
of his missing two front teeth

so clear, I had to sit
for a minute, on someone else's porch.

Four years since Riley died;
since the tsunami hit Japan—

all those children swept away.
You'd think we'd heal, yet today,

at our younger son's game,
as Desmond raced toward home,

his father cheered, *Go Riley!*
We stared at one another,

seeing our first son
fall all over again—

skull of memory cracked open
against concrete.

Ode to the Crossing Guard at 25ᵗʰ & Pearl

Braving speeding vehicles all day,
with just her body and a feeble stick—
lofting one word, *STOP.*

When a car struck, splaying me
in a cross walk, years ago,
on this very date, April 28,

Where were you? I wonder,
when the guard's eyes meet mine.

Drivers rush to work, check emails,
apply last-minute mascara—

A toddler in a tutu escapes
her mother's grasp, just as a minivan

breeches the crosswalk—brakes screeching
as the guard wings her arms,
then leads the girl to the curb.

She waves us on,
blond hair illuminating her face
like St. Gianna's aureole.

Night Bleed

I don't remember what book
I read to him
or which striped pajamas he wore.

I remember him waking to use
the bathroom, his face in the hallway—
eyes half-mast.

I don't remember how long
it took him to fall asleep
or if I was short with him.

I remember hoping
he wouldn't wake again
until morning.

I don't remember how often
he asked for water,
or climbed out of bed.

I remember the guttural sound
coming from his room—a cross between
a seal's bark and a human grunt.

I don't remember
kissing him goodnight.

I remember worrying
he had croup.

I don't remember
pulling the blanket
over his body.

I remember finding him
in his bed on all fours,
like a woman in labor.

I don't remember the moment
he fell asleep.

I remember yelling for him
to come back.

I don't remember
turning off his light.

What I'm Holding in the Black and White Photo of Me and My First-Born Son

Neither of us smiles.

I cradle his body, left arm snug
across his back, right arm slung below his legs.

> *I think I'm holding hours of night,*
> *sleepless motherhood,*
> *the mistakes of labor.*

My thumb rests
on the side of his head,
over the hidden birth defect.

> *I haven't discovered I'm holding the time bomb*
> *of his death.*

Behind us, looming ficus trees,
streaks of gray sky. My chin touches
his soft fontanel.

> *I don't know I'm holding his malformed vessels,*
> *a tsunami of blood.*

My blond hair veils my weary face.

> *I can't see I'm holding lost time,*
> *wasted breast milk.*

He looks away from the camera,
toward something I don't see.

> *Now, I realize I'm holding my scar tissue,*
> *a capsule, the open air. Time.*

Sleepover

As the sun auto-pilots
down the French windows,
I hear feet thumping,
running around upstairs,
a bedroom door closing.

Desmond and a boy play
in the room he used to share
with his brother, Riley,
before he died.

My husband returns from work,
his dropped change chiming,
on the tile counter.

I empty Desmond's lunch bag,
trash the gnawed apple,
remove a paper airplane
nosedived in the cat's water bowl.

Upstairs, the boys
build a fort from chairs
and cardboard, whisper beneath
a faded blanket, emitting
an occasional screech.

I flip through a magazine
at our kitchen table;
my husband scrolls
through emails on his iPhone.

Their voices reach us,
from the faraway island
of forgotten normalcy,
their laughter humming
like a familiar engine—
our family car's tire gone flat,
but given a spare.

What We Choose to Believe

All of Spain feels the infinite sadness of Julen's family.
          —Spanish Prime Minister Pedro Sánchez

They've survived a year
in the black hole of grieving—

their three-year-old son's
death from a rare heart condition.

I've lost a young son too,
and know the depth

of their sorrow's chasm.
They're spooning paella on plates

for a picnic, when they hear
their two-year-old son screaming,

as he falls into an actual hole,
an abyss sized just for him.

Days later, rescue crews
drill through rock—

but most likely he is smothered in dirt
and broken,

though his mother wants to believe
he is cradled whole in a blanket of air.

If it's true there is a God up there,
help him please,

she posts on day three,
with a photo of a sleeping baby.

When rescuers reach him
ten days later,

I can only be grateful
he didn't survive
the two hundred-foot fall
to die slowly of injury,

hunger, and dehydration—
both of Victoria and Jose's sons

in the same black hole
with my dead son,

whole only in their mothers'
grief, another word for *love*.

All three smothered in dirt
but cradled by

a blanket of air.

Mustela Baby Wipes

remind me of Riley,
writhing on the changing pad,

my willowy silhouette
wrestling his thrusting legs—

wisp of hair bookmarked
behind my ear.

The memory scrapes
like a skipping record—

hoist his bum,
clutch his kicking legs,
wipe and repeat—

his brown eyes
plugged into mine

like a lifeline—
the Mustela scent

clinging to my tongue.
Its saccharine aftertaste,
masking his decay.

I Want to Be Kind to My Seven-Year-Old Son

When Desmond plays handball indoors,
while brushing his teeth.

When he knocks down a picture with the ball,
on the way to grab his backpack.

When he asks, *Mommy, can I have some water?*
Mommy, can I tell you something?

When I warn, *You're going to be late for school,*
and he delays, *Wait, I have to get something—*

as he throws the socks he almost put on
across the room, and my chest tightens.

When he returns with a football,
Just One Hail Mary. It will be quick.

When I bellow, *No!*—my need
to control, cinching like a corset.

When he grabs my iPhone, *Siri,*
tell my mom to let me throw a Hail Mary.

When I force one deep breath
after another.

When he ties, unties, reties,
then double-knots his shoes.

When he says, *I know you're annoyed with me,*
because you're breathing loud.

When I remember being seven,
with my own agenda, and unconscious breath.

When he imitates my breathing,
to make me laugh.

When the corset unravels
like loose thread.

III.

At the Hair Salon Today

A boy slumps sideways
in a wheelchair,
a breathing tube
attached to his mouth
like an umbilical cord.

He has the same look
Riley had, after blood leaked
into his brain,
from the defective vessel—
a short-circuited robot,
a zombie, a ghost.

The boy wears gray socks
with rockets blasting off
that Riley would have liked.

What it's like
to lose a child only partially,
to live with his spirit trapped
deep in his body—
a wheeling billboard for tragedy.

I only had a glimpse,
the night Riley died.

I confess,
I want him whole
or not at all.

This slumping boy's mother
reads *People Magazine,*
while the stylist
smooths her hair,
with a flat iron,
and the nurse assures him,
Your mama be right back, mi amor.
She adjusts his body and head
to make him straighter.

Desmond's Older Brother Is

A blank space on the family tree
Desmond fills in for homework.

Old photos fading on our kitchen wall.

A question
he doesn't like to answer.

A secret confession
to a friend in class.

A book of poems
he doesn't want to read.

A canceled playdate.

Memories
he can't remember.

The vanilla milk Desmond likes to buy,
but never drinks.

A candle on our fireplace mantel.

Younger than he is now.

While Cleaning the Playroom

Nestled between his dusty baseball glove
and Darth Vader mask,
I find the cast Riley saved
from his broken arm.

I remember how,
running to tell me something,
he fell, left limb caught
oddly underneath his torso,
like a snapped tree branch—

his first and only break,
the year before he died.

I couldn't stand
even a part of him damaged,
but he wore his cast
like that Darth Vader mask,

hoisting his light saber skyward
to show his friends.

When the doctor removed the cast,
the speeding, circular blade
spun as close to his skin
as a stone skimming water.

Riley placed the cast on the shelf,
its neon orange body split in two,

like a part of himself
he would no longer need.

I fit the halves together,
an orange shell,
frayed at the wrist.

When Desmond Asks, *Am I Born to Play Football?*

It's violent and brutish, I want to say.
Grown men crashing into each other,
like souped-up monster trucks,
as spectators roar like Romans at the Colosseum.
Torn hamstrings, dislocated shoulders.
Ruptured discs, cracked skulls,
blood leaking like gasoline.

I want to say he can never play it.
Ever!

But when he faithfully practices
his pigskin spin in the yard—

I see the way his face lights up,
like Lambeau Field on opening night.

Proxy

It's an ivory trophy

Desmond's brother

never received.

Nights of careful brushing,

flossing in the mirror.

Months of waiting

for the empty space to fill.

His awkward apple bites,

his tongue's resting place,

his brother's proxy.

Thinnest Day of the Year

When our older son Riley died,

my husband touched a tree to see if it was real.

Six years later, on Halloween, our surviving son, Desmond,

turns the yard surreal,

with Halloween zombie heads,

severed feet, and tombstones.

The leaves on the neighbor's ficus blacken.

Mold grows on our shower tiles' grout.

Canker sores fester in my mouth.

When I drive Desmond to school, the parking lot

is empty. *Where is everybody?* he asks.

A stranger's voice answers my husband's phone

when I call him at the gym,

He wants me to tell you he's okay,

but there's been an accident . . .

Decapitated heads and bloodied necks

glisten in daylight, severed hands reach

from earth, trying to pull themselves out.

I catch my reflection in a store window:

When did my skin become like ash?

Raising Grief

Mourning was born,
colicky, wet-eyed.
Trying to console her,
sleep-deprived,
I pushed her
in a stroller,
tried every octave.

Those first years
bled nights—
falling asleep
with her in my arms,
breathing in unison,
protecting the fontanel
on her fragile head.

Now, I know
to feed her sweet-bread,
and help her self-soothe
when she seethes.

Before she runs off
to climb a tree,
she nuzzles me
on a park bench,
swinging her legs
like a four-year-old.

Mother Trucker

Desmond keeps screeching at his video game
on the way to football practice,

> *Mother Trucker!*

> *What's the big deal?, he asks,*
> *I'm not saying, fucker.*

Riley never spoke that word.
They're just words,
I used to tell my mother
when she yelled,
I should wash your mouth with soap!

I'm mother trucking down
a real highway to Hell,
bumper to bumper,
horns blaring—

> *Dammit, he head-shotted me!*
> Desmond yells at his *Fortnite* Hell,

as bicycles whir by
my bird-shat window,

and afternoon traffic
and motherhood
head-shot me.

I swerve a lane, wishing for an app like Waze,
to help navigate my journey.

Should I turn left,
on Lenient Lane,
or make a sharp right,
on Rigid Road?

> *I got three kills!*

I scowl in my rearview mirror,

as he tries to head-off judgment,

> *Don't worry . . . there's no blood,*

and I wonder if I missed a short-cut.

> *Just one more round . . .*
> *I'll go to tilted towers and die . . .*

Should I veer left
or make a U-turn at Unplug Way?

> *Mother Trucker!*

When traffic stops,
and I slam on the brakes—

> *Mom, you made me die!*

His words whiplash,
like a rear-ending bus,
I'm trucking him up—

> *in Fortnite,* he reassures,
> *not real life.*

Some other mother in a Porsche Cayenne,
breezes by and cuts me off.

Mother Trucker! I yell

> *Mom, really? She looks nice.*

She probably doesn't allow her kids
to play video games, I say,

as if I could bypass the hazards,
or navigate away
from the same dead end,

where it's not
the trucking mother's fault.

Reflection

After DaShaun Washington

with each September step
I rustle the dead
my son's ghost hides
behind a sycamore
the tree clings to her foliage
like a lost child
I glimpse his mother
in a store window
steel eyes of a crow
stare back and wither
her lemon-dry hair

God's Hand

Scaling a wall at the beach,
Desmond slips—and falls—
thwacking muscle and bone
against concrete.

I imagine internal bleeding,
fractured spine, paralysis.

When his older brother died,
faith in children's resilience
abandoned me.

A friend indicted me,
You should have left him
on life support longer:
God gives miracles—

I think of the Texas teen,
who fell thirty-five hundred feet
skydiving and survived—

her spine, pelvis, and two ribs
broken in half; her lungs, liver,
and brain bleeding—but alive,

expected to make a full recovery—
her sister assured reporters,
God's hand caught her.

My son jumps up like a puppet,
I'm okay, Mommy!
I'll never get hurt.
Me Hulk, he says,
pounding his chest.

I want to believe him.

Clear-Cut

It falls from my binder,
cherry crayon streaks
ripen in sun, *LOVE RILEY*—

a valentine from my son,
three weeks before he died,

cutout paper once a tree,
before its felling,
and reduction to pulp.

I pick up the heart,
hold it like a seed I'll save

to grow an oak.
I couldn't answer
his question,

Mommy, does paper
remember being a tree?

A Different Clock

I used to bring my boys
to this park to swing—

lulled at first,
by the tick-tock

of their feet rising to sky,
and falling to earth.

I sat on the grass—
growing restless,

as my watch's hour-hand
slackened at noon.

They never wanted to leave,
always another rock to throw,

another grassy hill,
to fling their bodies down,

nowhere else
they needed to be,

as measured by
their boyish clocks.

My clock shows me
my blond toddler, standing

with his older brother,
faces tilted skyward

to watch a plane take off,
and arrow away.

My second-hand paces
with my husband on the path

mid-thirties, baseball cap,
no phone in his hand yet,

smiling easily.
He says something to me—

I can't hear, as I look through
the wrong end of a telescope;

push one son
in a stroller down the path,

sunlight flickers
through branches

like a short-circuiting cord,
my older son skipping ahead

to his diagnosis,
his nothingness to come.

To the Frustrated Mother in Starbucks with Her Three-Year-Old Son

Don't worry. One day he will
stop hitting you when he's mad,
hands swatting at your face,
like a short-circuited robot.

He will stop throwing himself
on floors, and thrashing
his head like a punk rocker,
when you tell him, *No.*

Some day he will stop
running outdoors every time
he sees a mangy pigeon,
bobbing along the sidewalk,

leaving you to spill coffee,
and chase him, grabbing
his shirt, just before he steps
into moving traffic.

You probably won't notice
when he stops. You'll be
too busy, helping him trace
his uppercase letters, playing

game after game of Roshambo,
listening to his knock-knock jokes.
You'll be too busy answering
his questions, *Mommy,*

can I tell you something?
Mommy, can I have gummy bears?
Mommy, who was the first
person on earth?

You probably won't remember
when he turned three,
till you see another mother
with her three-year-old—

her jaw tense, her hand
clutching his arm,
as he pulls her hair
with his freakishly strong fist.

By then, your son will be standing
in line beside you, ordering
Iced Caramel Macchiato,
his large hands hanging at his sides.

Then, you will remember
him small in your lap,
one hand holding your finger,
the other pointing at a balloon,
Mommy, Boom!

When My Yoga Teacher Tells Me I'm Vata Deranged

I can think of worse things.

It's windy in your head, she says,

but I like the soughing in my mind.

Thoughts blow through me like clouds.

Words loft like helium bags, swirling

along my shoreline, then settling.

My sister's having a baby,

I need to buy more vanilla milk,

breeze through me like a simoon.

Does my dead son climb trees in heaven?

The squall in my head

knocks down memory lines,

fractures and uproots grief,

wrenches time from its hinges.

Tranquility is overrated,

stillness weak.

I dive, tumble, then soar on my gritty, muscular wind.

Acknowledgments

Thank you to Alexis Rhone Fancher, Karin Gutman, Tresha Haefner, and April Ossman. A special thank you to Tom Lombardo and Kevin Watson. My deepest gratitude to my husband, Lee, for his unwavering support, and to my sons, Desmond and Riley, for continuing to be a source of joy and inspiration.

Chanel Brenner

Chanel Brenner is the winner of the 2021 Press 53 Award for Poetry for *Smile, or Else*. She is the author of *Vanilla Milk: A Memoir Told in Poems*, (Silver Birch Press, 2014), which was a finalist for the 2016 Independent Book Awards and honorable mention in the 2014 Eric Hoffer awards. Her poems have appeared in *Rattle, Raleigh Review, New Ohio Review, Duende, Muzzle Magazine, Spry Literary Journal, Barrow Street, Salamander, Spoon River Poetry Review, Literary Mama*, and others. Her poem, "Apology," won first place in the Smartish Pace Beullah Rose Poetry Prize (2018) and her poem, "July 28th, 2012," won first prize in The Write Place At the Write Time's contest, judged by Ellen Bass. Her essays have appeared in *Modern Loss, The Good Men Project*, and *HerStry*. She lives in Southern California with her husband and son.